Earth's Dirtied Floor

George P. Deneff

Contents

Heaven 1

Welcome
My kingdom
You rightfully deserve

Hell 1

Welcome
My wasteland
You rightfully deserve

Heaven 2

as I'm making my way down this tranquil hallway
the feelings of timidness and uncertainty fall down hard
every stride is becoming wider and longer
with burnt charcoal and myrrh leading the way
the hugs and smiles are felt, but not visible at the moment
this warmth is undeniably the warmest I've experienced
warmth that forces you to love even your largest detractor
now approaching the 10 steps of his holiness
I kneel before it all, for permission to enter
I look up to witness
this giant figure emerging from behind his gate
free from hate, death, loss, hurt, contempt, question
his holiness grabs my face with fingertips hot to the touch
and calmly informs me in mesmerizing song
"take your sandals off and hang your sin on the coat rack
before you enter your new home"

goldened trumpeters continue

Hell 2

Hell's bell chimers lament

as I'm making my way down this disturbed hallway
the feelings of self-assurance and invincibility float high away
every stride is becoming more stiff and narrow
with burnt flesh and hopelessness leading the way
the daggering eyes and frowns are felt, but not visible at the moment
this icy chill is undeniably the coldest I've experienced
chill that forces you to fear even your most vulnerable prey
now approaching the 10 steps of his wickedness
I cower before it all, imploring to leave
I peak up to witness
this shadowed figure lurking from behind his gate
full of hate, death, loss, hurt, contempt, question
his wickedness grabs my face with pointed talons burning to the touch
and aggressively informs me in deranged song
"get used to your rusted shackles and leave your hope on the coat rack before you enter your
new home"

Hell's bell chimers continue

Heaven 3

all hope found
no more cries
given peace
truth no lies

spirits pray
wings that glow
love my view
watch below

you could have
been with me
you chose hate
refused he

time will tell
where you stay
twisted minds
bombs away

Hell 3

all hope lost
too much pain
given time
it's insane

demons feast
wings don't sing
hate my view
I'm no king

I could have
been with you
I chose hate
life I threw

time will tell
where I stay
what regret
look away

Heaven 4

Peter passes me the purest bread
Andrew gives me a bite of cleanly scaled fish to try
James squeezes my shoulders uncle-like before he seats himself
John tells the table a joke he heard for the very first time
Philip pours freshly pressed wine in our encrusted goblets
Bartholomew sits next to me radiating joy and relief from any sorrows
Matthew cuts the lamb straight down the middle for all who care to join in
Thomas kisses the brutally purpled feet of those who carry bruises
James sits quietly and takes in what I take in; sheer delight
Simon made an apricot marmalade that goes quite well with this bread
Thaddeus suggests we hold hands and repent for the sins occurring without break
Judas Iscariot is nowhere to be seen

Hell 4

Jack the Ripper sits feasting on organ meats of the damned
Dahmer rips in to his well done cut of ribs
Shipman sweats yellow beads worrying he'll be one-upped
Gacy applies his makeup, grins in his pocket-sized mirror, wipes it all off, repeats
Holmes will be late for supper because of some final tweaks to his newest torture device
Hitler is carving swastikas all over his body like a possessed animal
Bundy holds his mouth wide open to sink his teeth into freshly deposited souls
Stalin curls his mustache anxiously awaiting his follicles to finally give
Himmler picks a seat next to Hitler, and just exudes contempt for it all
Ramirez hobbles over to the table with crutches that are super-glued to his foul pits
Genghis Khan has many ideas he feels he'll be pursuing in the near future
Satan screeches a tumultuous scream that quiets even the craziest bastard

this picture is just right
starry skies that flood the night
blue jays chirp a tune that's tight
my silly tears are restrained through might
a couple little boys start a snowball fight
a few gold cherubs skipping along with a clean kite
no need for a tall, armored knight
the baker in the stained glass window shares a sweetly frosted bite
the maker reaches out and pulls forth the depth of light
these eyes that were blinded once are shown freedom of sight
my canvas was a blank slate that pretended to stay white
a clean life I lived gives me the ability to take flight

this picture is not right
bloody hands that paint the night
vicious hellhounds bark satanic sounds making one clench tight
salted tears flow down honest with all my might
a couple little boys bleed out their mother in a fight
a few red demons scurry fast with their stolen kite
much need for a tall, armored knight
the baker in the fogged up window consumes 7 layers in every bite
the faker reaches out and pulls down the shades blocking desperate light
these eyes that remain blinded prefer to possess an absence of sight
my canvas was a black slate that pretended to be white
a filthy life I lived ripped the wings that were needed for my limitless flight

Heaven 6

I helped
I prayed
I kneeled
I forgave
I believed
I encouraged
I loved
I gave

Hell 6

I hindered
I renounced
I stood
I blamed
I doubted
I discouraged
I hated
I incaved

Heaven 7

this ghastly ghetto isn't for me
please, for god's sake, make me free!
I can't bear the smells of my roasting siblings
why, oh why, is your light not bright enough to see?

shrieks and screams quiver the greenest tree
mama and I are next in line to meet thee
I feel cold; I'm too cold to cry my final tears
please, I'll never return; haven't I paid the greatest fee?

Hell 7

this ghetto-labor camp was built for me!
I can't help but laugh when they make a plea!
meat hooks, experiments, starvation
one by one tossed in my oven struggling to flee!

arms wailing for survival is something to see!
flames engulf a huddling family of three!
I control who'll live or die in my camp
too bad I can't torture their souls risen free...

Heaven 8

Christians press their holy palms together for a gentle prayer
Muslims pull out the Persian rug and slap their palms into the earth
Jews put on proper attire out of respect for their high holy Sabbath
this holy trinity totally blind to their unification set in stone from the start of it all
these holy wars so brutal and unnecessary for the purpose of an ignorant superiority complex
ignorance is never bliss because of the disastrous repetition of sin we strive to further continue
just like we have different foods and music in the world to enjoy and share,
we practice different religions to accommodate the differences of cultures
but to come together as one is the fundamental goal down to these sturdy roots
even though our directions take us on different streets and freeways,
we all meet up at the same destination

Hell 8

Luciferians light their candles in the Sigil of Baphomet before black mass
Diabolists travel the streets casting spells and black magic curses on the innocent
Demonists put on their black robes with smoothly red-painted faces to worship true evil
this diabolical trio completely content with their followers from all demonic denominations
they work together to demolish purity and peace that dare contest their devious missions
missions that succeed because they penetrate with harder, faster bullets
mental illness, disease, torture, disharmony, war, poor
these issues exist not because that's the way it's meant to be,
but because while the holy religions fight and tear down each other,
this diabolical trio work together to stab the weakened backs on top of a ridiculous dog pile
when we stop acting like fools, stand up straight, and dust each other off
the light we all share becomes painfully bright instead of pitifully dim
our uncensored light will explode throughout every crevice and scare the darkest of shadows

Heaven 9

Through thick grass
Seen afar
A lost pup
High thigh scar

Patched him up
Gave last drink
No one cared
Life can stink

Hell 9

Through dark grass
Seen afar
A dumb dog
Weak from scar

Cut out tongue
Made taco
What a find
Mind's wacko

Heaven 10

I saw him! I felt his warmth!
standing in my kitchen in confusion
I suddenly have the taste of charcoal on my tongue
as I'm trying to wash my mouth out with water
he appears in front of me head to toe in a burlap robe
his brown sandals are aged as much as his wisdom
I can't help but bow down to him and beg for forgiveness
I grab his coarse ankles and feel what it means to truly repent
all my wrongdoings along with every sin I've done and will do
my eyes blind me with tears welling up beyond my control
this energy forces me to cry out every last drop of sadness
he gently grabs my cheeks and points for me to look around
I wipe my eyes with the back of my mortal hands
and I can see 40 hooded beings with their heads down
just surrounding me with compassion and understanding
as I look back at this immortal being
he helps me on my feet and stares deep through my eyes
I try to study his face, but it is invisible to the living
he pulls me in and hugs me firmly for a long time
the longest I've ever had
I continue to weep as I can feel him
absorbing my fears and troubles

I saw them… I felt it…
waking up drenched in cold sweat
my heartbeat is in a panic right away
as I open the window to let some cool air in
I sense the air is void of its typical scent
it smells like nothing; it smells colorless
this air doesn't even feel right
the texture is all off!
panic ensues once more and nausea now joins in
I quickly shut the window and grab yesterday's clothes off the chair and throw them on
ignoring my bladder screaming for some morning relief
I slowly walk downstairs not knowing what to expect
not halfway down the staircase
the corner of my eyes spot red orbs
there are about 8 of them
mildly bobbing up and down
like a bobber on a fishing line rests in calm waters
studying them carefully
they don't look very threatening
starting to believe I'm in a dream
playing this out until I wake is my only option
I feel my symptoms are put on simmer
so I continue to the kitchen to make some breakfast
and bring it in the living room to watch the news
"In a crowded mall in the state of Washington, 72 were killed and 167 severely injured by 8
masked men who wore explosives strapped around their stomachs…"
pain so real and sharp gutted me like a worthless trout
that simmering flame went to high heat immediately
letting me know I am very much awake...

Heaven 11

That damn gunner got me real good
I should have seen him and withstood
My one wish could never be
To live through this for my babies
An old grandpa through my eighties
Liver, kidneys, spilt on me

Hell 11

An easy target crawling low
Bullets are fast; I prefer slow
Here lies my foe, taking aim
Dumb bastard's tears will cause a miss
Trembling and sobbing in his piss
Organs in bits; lives I claim

Heaven 12

Staring up at the 21st floor

I stare at the same spot everyday passing
could my life be this bad? am I done breathing and lasting?
I suppose being molested by two pigs for uncles is enough to quit
my priest with the golden robe and fancy jewelry who would ask me to sit
therapy wasn't capable of eliminating the emotions that reside deep within my locked cage
climbing higher and higher in my career hasn't suppressed my demons no matter the wage
unconditional love is never unconditional unless you're one of the gods
I'm ok with love that you have to earn; prices must be paid to even the most innocent of dogs
the only thing that keeps me off that alluring building with shattered windows is a family
Earth is a jacked up place with too much evil, and I'm compelled to spread hope and humility

Hell 12

Staring down from 21 stories up

strong wind currents blow through my oily hair
darkened clouds converge too quick to bear
the freezing temperature strips my body naked
this vulnerability once held vise-tight is no longer sacred
please forgive me, the ones I choose to forget
and let me try another option for peace I couldn't get
it's not unconditional love that has failed me
but love and support that for many others was never a guarantee
as I ready myself to fly down in the perfect formation of a beautiful bird
remember me as a sensitive human being that cared too much, who wasn't absurd

Heaven 13

my grandmother and I would sit for hours and listen
to the sweet sounds of the charmante Lucienne Boyer
even though her record was scratched and hissed
it added genuine quality you wouldn't understand
unless you sat in this room
and saw the sheer joy
my modest grandmother showed
while knitting her
tributes for
Grandfather

she told me once about these encounters at her grandparents'
you see, she would go up every summer break
into a rural town of approximately 150 people
where her grandparents owned 10 square acres
they sent her to the grocer
to buy milk and eggs
only she was stopped
stripped by 3
her last
encounter

Born is the sacrificial lamb to be
Born is the golden baby delivered by our mighty king
Born is Mary's baby, Mary's downfall, Mary's blessing
Born is our father, our protector, our salvation
Bring him the best herbs and animals around
Bring him temporary comfort, a baby's cap, a baby's crib
Bring him your lies and deliver him your truths
Bring him your soul and never ask him for proof

Born is the fallen angel to be
Born is the red furry beast delivered by our mighty king
Born is the evil, the cruel, the volatile
Born is our doom, our tormenter, our fallen king
Bring him the lost souls and the abusers of God's virginal children
Bring him forever torture, complete agony, total loss
Bring him your lies and bring him what you deny
Bring him your filthy soul that is too heavy to rise

Heaven 15

I am forced to bear memories that weren't my creations
My forefathers' fathers entrust me with every member's personal keepsafe
They let me dine with them and taste the family kept recipes
With their cherished past come the horrors passed down through many generations

The checkered blanket picnics I've been invited on destroyed by strafe
Many friends of theirs were introduced to me, as well as their worst enemies
Witnessing one cousin march out to fight the Peloponnesian War
As my other pathetic cousin murders the helpless and keeps the cobblestone paths unsafe

The history channel is way off on what they believe are factual documentaries
I have been shown the truth of it all, the way life really unfolds; helping hands to silent gore
The worst memory I was privy to was the raping of my 16th century aunt awaiting her miserable hearse
Why do I need to be tormented day by day by reliving my ancient relatives' memories?

Maybe I was born for much more?
Maybe birthed to hold the depressing truths that fracture my core?
Possibly spawned by the underworld with a predestined curse?
Possibly the more I say, the less they'll disperse?

Hell 15

My mind carries chrome gears that sit brand new
They might as well be cracked and rusty
For this mind is stagnant like a toxic swamp
Never having the pleasure of experiencing a loose screw

Odors from this softened skull create an atmosphere that's musty
Emotions mid-level create a safe feeling that make one almost stomp
To always envy the eccentrics, the creatives, the thinkers, the innovators
Is enough to be finished with normalcy and take up arms when the weather isn't too gusty

Why wasn't I raised to eat my polite meals with great fervor, with the mightiest chomp?
K-12 taught me if I achieved straight A's, life would be an ocean's breeze and I could be the best of all imitators
I'd rather be found ass up face down in the gutter of a lightless street than be genuinely worshipped for false fame
All that exists beneath this well dressed, clean shaven man, is a sad man who'll never muster up the courage to be seen clomp

Maybe I was born to install boxy refrigerators?
Maybe I am not going to be remembered as being one of the great originators?
Possibly spawned from a loving place to exist like one and the same?
Possibly the more I try to exclaim, the less I'll continue to blame?

Heaven 16

I whistled a tune
A flock of birds cared to join
We whistle as one

I whistled a tune
The smallest of birds flew by
They rejected me

Heaven 17

There, there
You're safe with me
We traveled light-years to be
Created from galaxies away and stored right here
Your mom's little house secures you
With your first breath
It's filtered

There, there
Would you hold still
This will taint you darkened forever
But with the dark lord we will thrive
You will grow to loathe everyone
And pursue evil endeavors
You're welcome

Heaven 18

Creativity is a blessing and a curse
To create is to temporarily alleviate your ailments and possibly cure someone else's
The most beautiful creations are not possible without the aid of the ugliest demons
Sounds of angels flying off the enlightening violin strings have evil fiends screeching behind the scenes
Breathtaking pieces of innovative artwork aren't a reality without bouts of disillusionment and schizophrenia lending a hand
Trouble conjuring up new ideas and groundbreaking revelations aren't relatable to those who create from deep angst
This paralyzing anxiety and petrified fright propel the art world to heights that aren't possible without these unfortunate elements
In a way, the saying "take a negative and turn it into a positive" really isn't a corny quote from some guy full of shit
The purpose of evil is to torment, devastate, destroy, mutilate, discourage, and just completely make life unbearable
But the strongest of God's army are cycled through life many times over to bear the brunt of it all
To pick up the painter's brush
To place the fine horse hairs on the strings
To type the words that create turbulent emotion

Hell 18

Creating has taken the greatest toll on me
What once released endorphins and stress
Only keeps my cortisol sky-high and demons bottled up inside
I cannot create at the level of my unrealistic standards without the help of Lucifer
He gives me a strange gift that cuts away at me day by day
This knife has always carved away at my soft organs and hardened skin
But eventually the body and mind are missing too much to not notice
The first class accommodations and finest champagnes were numbing agents
They blinded me into thinking life was all good
When in reality
It's only those who reap my benefits
That truly are living the good life
I now acknowledge I probably signed a pact with the devil
And I candidly realize it will be the cause of my struggling blood bath
The strange thing is God was there with the devil and I
As all three of us signed our names on the dotted line of this little document
I guess I willingly participated in being the sacrificial lamb
For the sake of propelling mankind forward into some light
Light that faked being bright for me
What I fail to understand
Is why Lucifer helps out in any way
And why God signs off on these perverse ordeals

Heaven 19

A baby caressed in my arm,
as my oldest child holds my hand.
I lock up the room and we walk
downstairs to the lobby to get some snacks.
Every Friday night is movie night with us.
Ever since their father walked out for good,
my oldest dwells less on his bad moods
when he's watching *Toy Story* or *Small Soldiers.*

I pay for the snacks and we head back up to the room.
My son is jumping up and down repeatedly in excitement.
I tell him to relax in a stern, but jovial tone.
I know he's not going to stop jumping,
and deep down, I don't want him to.

I unlock the door knob and walk on over
to the counter to take out the snacks.
I give my son his bag of Whoppers,
and I put my baby on her gently cleaned blanket,
with little pink and light blue bubble prints all over.

Is everyone all set for the movie?
"Yes Mom, play it, play it!"
So I press play and sink into the sofa.
As they watch *Toy Story* for the eightieth time,
I'll try to watch it from beginning to end for the first time.

As they sit and stare at the TV screen,
I sit and stare at them for most of the movie.
Their baby cherub faces exist for only a short time,
and I intend on enjoying every second of it.

Hell 19

My child! My baby!
I only went down to the lobby for a minute.
To break a five for a pack of Black Marlboros.
Leaving my eight year old son in charge of my newborn
was a terrible mistake!
A life altering mistake!
An unforgivable mistake!

My babies! Why! Why! God, why!
My son was left to watch the oven.
I told him when it was close to finished,
to turn the dial off when it smells well done.
I was only gone for maybe ten minutes most.
I don't understand!

Lord! Son of a God Damn Bitch!
While in front of our building taking a drag,
I start to smell the stench of a foreign odor.
I cup my hands and light my cigarette;
taking a puff, laughing at someone's failed dinner plans.
Little did I know,
I was smelling the life burning out of my innocent babies.

Ahhhhhhhhhhhhhhhhhhhhhh!
Ahhhhhhhhhhhhhhhhhhhhhhh!
The yells and cries of my babies
are heard from the open window.
Save them! Somebody save them!
I try to run back into the complex,
but the stairs are engulfed in black smoke,
as the elevator's electrical circuit is broken.
It's been broken for the last two years...

Fire engines are heard
Frantically running around screaming,
I grab my neighbors' shocked faces,
begging for anyone to help me get up to my babies.
They all brush me off and tell me,
"Lady, I'm sorry, but whoever's still in there are goners."
I swing my fists around my body trying to deck their smug expressions,
but they only block it and stare at me with pity, pathetic pity.

Firefighters barge into the building and break through the barriers I created.
The large hoses are being rushed over to shower the dancing flames.
Ten minutes go by, and the fire is finally put out.
I grab the heroic men by the collars of their tired uniforms,
and beg them to let me see my saved children;
my innocent, precious children.
They give each other a discouraging glance.
"Mam, we're sorry, your babies were fused together
huddled in a corner as charred as we've ever seen."

My child... My baby...

Heaven 20

In my triple-sheeted bed I lay
Wise crickets know just what to say
Brilliant stars force peace to be upon me tonight
This pillow case is refreshingly cold and right
Deep sleep from the purple skies evoke an urge to pray

Hell 20

In a ripped up cot I lay
Peaceful sleep is only a dream for another day
Strange creaking from the oak panel floor alarms me
The new kid preys upon the weak who will quickly agree
This isn't temporary housing; this is a perpetual buffet